THE
FRIENDLY
SNOWFLAKE

M. SCOTT PECK, M.D.

THE FRIENDLY SNOWFLAKE

A Fable of

Faith, Love and Family

Illustrated by

CHRISTOPHER SCOTT PECK

Ariel Books

Turner Publishing, Inc.

ATLANTA

Dedicated to
Ian Christopher Gingrich
and
Armand Eisen

—MSP and CSP

THE FRIENDLY SNOWFLAKE
A Fable of Faith, Love and Family

Published by Turner Publishing, Inc.
A Subsidiary of Turner Broadcasting System, Inc.
One CNN Center, Box 105366
Atlanta, Georgia 30348-5366

First Edition
10   9   8   7   6   5   4   3
ISBN 1-878685-28-7
ISBN 1-878685-30-9   10 Shelf Counter Unit
Library of Congress Catalog Card Number 92-61199

Distributed by Andrews and McMeel
4900 Main Street
Kansas City, MO 64112

Produced by Ariel Books
Art Direction: Armand Eisen and Michael Hortens
Design: Diane Stevenson

foreword

For years people asked me to write a children's book, particularly one that would embody some of the principles of *The Road Less Traveled*. Always I replied, "I don't know how to talk to children. You do it."

But in early November I went to lecture in Columbus, Ohio. I checked into my hotel room and sat looking out at the city. There had been a cold snap. While not stormy, the sky was lead gray. I missed home. The view was not uplifting, and I was feeling a bit sorry for myself. At that moment a solitary snowflake appeared in front of the window. "Hello, Snowflake," I addressed it. I marveled at the patience of its passage; it was so tiny and light. "It cheers me up to see you," I said. "It was nice of you to come by." Finally, as it drifted out of sight, I exclaimed, "Maybe you're a friendly snowflake!" And that was when this book was born.

A week later I told my son, Christopher, an artist, I had started writing my first book that would be for children as well as adults. He volunteered to illustrate it. So began a fortunate collaboration.

The most frequent of all questions I receive is from parents—often disinterested in Sunday School or the like—who ask, "What should I do for the spiritual education of my children?"

"First, love them," I reply. "Next, read to them. Stories. Lots of stories." Being who I am, this is naturally a spiritual sort of story. It is meant to be read in such a way by young people with old souls and older people with young souls.

M. Scott Peck, M.D.
Bliss Road
New Preston, CT 06777

THE
FRIENDLY
SNOWFLAKE

Just after Halloween it turned cold. So cold her mother made Jenny put on her heavy sweater and gloves before she went out to play in the meadow. Jenny didn't like being bundled up. She wanted to be as free as summer.

Still she could run, and when she reached the meadow, Jenny dashed to the middle of the field. She was about to throw herself down on the tall brown hay when she noticed that each stalk was stiff with frost from the night. She stopped. It would be like jumping onto a bed of little spears. Maybe her mother had been right to bundle her up.

The sky was gray, as gray as the granite boulders that dotted the meadow. Jenny looked up to see a tiny snowflake lazily drifting toward the ground. She peered at the pine trees at the far end of the meadow. She saw another little snowflake. Then another. They were so few and far apart that she could count them. *One. There's two. That's three over there. Four. Five. . . .*

Jenny had just counted to seventeen when she felt a quick, cold prickle on the tip of her nose. She made a face. Then she grinned as she realized she'd been so busy looking at the snowflakes in the distance she hadn't seen the one right on top of her. She pulled off her glove and touched the tip of her finger to where she'd felt the tingle. Yup, it was still wet where the little snowflake had melted on her skin.

Then she realized she had stopped counting. Where had she been? *Seventeen, that's right. No, eighteen.* That was counting the one that had surprised her nose. She slipped

10

her glove back on and looked toward the pine trees to start counting again. Only there weren't any more snowflakes to count. She looked and looked, but there was not a one. She stood looking for a long time, but nothing happened. It had stopped snowing.

Jenny started to walk around the meadow. She wanted to see lots and lots of flakes, a real snowstorm. But there had only been a few, and the snow was quickly over. As she walked a thought came to her. Since there were so few snow-flakes, wasn't it something that one of them had managed to find its way right to the tip of her nose there in the middle of the huge meadow? *Why?* Maybe it had wanted to meet her. Maybe it was a friendly snowflake!

Jenny stopped to sit on one of the gray boulders, won-dering. *Wasn't it nice of the little snowflake to come all the way down from the heavens just to introduce itself?* That was very friendly. And she would be happy to be its friend. But friends knew each other's name. Hers was Jenny. What was the snowflake's? As soon as she asked, Jenny knew. It was Harry. She couldn't tell anyone *how* she knew. She even thought about other names: Robert, Suzie, Adelaide, Parker. Nope, none of them fit. The friendly snowflake's name was Harry. She just knew.

Jenny was so excited. She wanted to tell someone about Harry. She could tell her older brother, Dennis, but he would laugh at her for giving the snowflake a name. *No, better not tell him about Harry's name.* But she could at least tell him about their meeting and how friendly it had been.

11

Jenny raced home to find Dennis, as usual, playing with the computer. He might have told her to shut up, but it was almost lunchtime and he was bored, so he listened to her tell him about the friendly snowflake.

"That's silly," he said when she finished. "Snowflakes aren't friendly."

"Well, this one was," Jenny countered. She was glad she hadn't told him about Harry's name.

"Snowflakes aren't friendly," Dennis insisted. "They just land where they land. It was an accident."

"It might have been if there'd been lots of snowflakes," Jenny retorted, "but there were only about twenty. I counted them. Just think. Only twenty snowflakes in the whole meadow, and one of them found me!"

12

"It didn't *find* you, stupid. It just happened to land on you," Dennis pronounced. "It was just a statistical happening."

Jenny looked at him angrily. He was twelve years old and thought he knew everything. She didn't know what *statistical* meant, but she could guess. "You think you're so smart," she snorted. "It was too . . . too special to just *happen*."

"No, it wasn't. It was just an accident," Dennis repeated. "It had no meaning."

"Yes, it did. It was not an accident!" Jenny's voice was rising.

"Yes, it was."

"No, it wasn't."

"Yes, it was!"

"No, it wasn't!"

Their mother heard them shouting from all the way in the kitchen. She marched into the living room. "What's all this fuss about?" she asked.

Jenny explained about the snowflake, carefully leaving out that she'd given it a name. "Tell her she's stupid, Mom," Dennis said as soon as she finished.

"I'll tell her no such thing," their mother addressed him.

Thinking she might have her mother on her side, Jenny insisted once more, "The snowflake was friendly. It wanted to meet me."

"It was just an accident," Dennis shot back.

"Children, children," their mother sighed. "It's really not worth arguing about, is it?"

Jenny stood her ground. "Yes, it is. It is worth arguing about. It's very important whether it was an accident or not."

Their mother looked at them thoughtfully. "You're right," she said after a moment. "It can be something worth arguing about. It's very important sometimes to decide whether something's an accident or whether there's meaning behind it. But in this case, neither of you has enough to go on to win the argument. So neither of you is going to be able to convince the other that you're right, are you?"

Jenny and Dennis didn't answer. She was right about that.

"So, I guess the question is whether you want to spend the rest of the day shouting at each other over something that can't be decided," their mother reasoned. "Is that what you want to do?"

Dennis shrugged and turned back to the computer. Their mother returned to the kitchen, and Jenny drifted out of the living room. It was going to be a long Sunday afternoon.

That night, when Jenny was in bed and all the lights were out, she wondered whether Harry liked her. He *must* have liked her to seek her out in the first place and be willing to melt on her nose. "I like you, too, Harry," she whispered just before falling asleep.

In the morning she was busy getting ready to go to school. Then she was busy with her friends on the school bus and busy in class. She was so busy all day that she totally forgot about Harry. For a while, that is.

14

chapter
✦ II ✦

Jenny awoke facing her bedroom window. It was snowing hard. Huge flakes were tumbling down, one upon another. She jumped out of bed and raced to get dressed. No school today. *It was Thanksgiving!* That afternoon, Uncle Ralph, her father's older brother, would be coming for dinner, and so would Aunt Martha and Gerald, their son, who was always so nice to her. But that wasn't the reason Jenny wanted to get up so early. She was in a hurry to be outside in the snow.

The front lawn had a thin film of white, as did the topsides of the tree branches. But past the lawn, the paved street was all black. As soon as each flake hit the tar, it vanished. Jenny groaned. The snow wasn't sticking. It was too warm.

Still, she had never seen such giant flakes. She ran to the side of the road and looked up at the sky. The flakes were so heavy they made her blink when they hit her face. Eyes closed, she tilted her head upward. *Splat. Splat. Splat,*

splat, splat. It almost felt like when she was taking a shower looking straight up at the nozzle.

She thought how different it had been with Harry. He had singled her out in the meadow; today, Jenny didn't feel that any of these flakes were seeking her out. But that didn't mean that they weren't friendly. Maybe they were all Harry's relatives.

Jenny wasn't sure this was true. These flakes were not at all like Harry. He had been so tiny, and these were so big. Jenny giggled. Maybe Harry was a little baby snowflake and these were grown-up snowflakes. She shook her head. Harry was not a baby. He was smart enough to find her. No, he was as old as she was, maybe even older.

Jenny sat down on the stone wall in front of the lawn and looked down the street. Whether or not these snowflakes were friendly, they were beautiful. They were so thick she couldn't even see to the end of the street where the road dipped toward the pine trees at the edge of the meadow. There was no wind, but the great flakes seemed to twirl around one another as they fell to earth. It was like they were all dancing with each other. Hard as she tried, Jenny couldn't keep her eyes on a single flake for more than a second or two; in their twirling dance, the snowflakes all became mixed up.

Maybe there was a way to look at them, she thought. Jenny noticed that when the flakes fell on her parka they seemed to stick there for a few seconds before they melted. She held her arm up in front of her face. *There's one!*

16

She examined it before it vanished. *There's another one!* She peered at it also. After looking closely at the third, she began to realize something: each huge flake seemed to have different parts to it.

17

Now Jenny looked even more closely. Yup, each one definitely had parts. In fact, each part looked like it might be a little snowflake itself. "Hey, that's it!" she said out loud. "I bet each big snowflake is actually a clump of little snowflakes!"

It was as if a whole bunch of Harrys had decided to stick together. *Why would they do that? Maybe they were related somehow.* Suddenly Jenny smiled. *That's it! Related.* "Each one of these large flakes is a family," she declared. "For all I know, one of them could even be Harry's family."

Jenny looked back to her sleeve to find more families. Suddenly a wet spot appeared on her parka where no flakes

18

had landed. Then another. And another. *Oh, no! Could these be raindrops?*

Jenny looked down the street again. The snow was not as thick now, and in between the white flakes she could make out gray raindrops. Even as she watched, the snowflakes became fewer and fewer, and the raindrops more and more. Darn. She tried to wish it backward, but it didn't work. Soon, it was almost all rain. And very wet. Jenny stood up and began to walk to the house. She felt like crying.

By the time she came inside, she was soaked. Her mother had her go upstairs for a hot shower. Dressed again, Jenny came downstairs to the living room, where Dennis was at the computer. "It stopped snowing," she announced glumly. "It's turned to rain."

"Ummm," her brother

nodded without looking up. At least he didn't tell her to go away.

"They were the biggest snowflakes I've ever seen," Jenny exclaimed. "They were gigantic!"

Now Dennis turned around and looked at her. He could never resist trying to teach her something. "It's not surprising the snow turned to rain," he said. "Snowflakes tend to be large when it's warmer than freezing."

"You know, when I looked closely," Jenny recounted, "each flake seemed to be a bunch of little flakes clumped together."

"Well, you're not so dumb after all," Dennis responded. "You're right. When it's warm and the flakes are about to melt, they get sticky. Sometimes that happens high up in the sky, but then it usually keeps snowing. Today, because it turned to rain, it was probably warmer down here, and they clumped together as they got close to earth."

19

Jenny didn't mind the lecture, even though Dennis was always so *factual*. "Anyway," she continued without mentioning Harry, "it's like each big flake was a family."

"Nah," Dennis snorted.

"Why not?"

"Because each flake is totally different. Here, let me show you." Her brother went over to the bookshelf to the

encyclopedia.
Dennis wanted to be
a scientist like their
father, so he was always
looking something up.
After a while he found the

right page and showed it to her. "That's how snowflakes look under a magnifying glass," he said.

There were a dozen pictures of snowflakes, each one very different. They were also, Jenny thought, very beautiful. Sometimes Jenny was glad her brother was so smart. But there was something off in his thinking. "Just because each little flake is different," she reasoned, "doesn't mean a big flake isn't a family."

"Nah. They clump together because they just happen to be next to each other in the air."

"Maybe they're next to each other because they're related," Jenny persisted.

"No, I told you they're each totally different. It's just an accident that they're next to each other."

Jenny thought for a moment. "Aren't you and I different?" she asked him. "And we're right here next to each other in the same living room. Is that an accident?"

Dennis looked uncomfortable. "No. Yes. Yes, we are different, and, yes, we are next to each other because we're related," he admitted.

"And isn't every human being different, just like every snowflake? And isn't every human part of somebody's

20

family?'' she went on. "So why can't each big snowflake be
a family?"

"Because it just *isn't,* stupid," Dennis insisted. "I told
you it's an accident."

It was Jenny's turn to snort. Only this time she was too
smart to push the argument into a shouting match. When-
ever there was something he didn't understand, Dennis
always called it an accident, as if that somehow explained
everything.

Later, sitting alone, she thought about how she loved
her brother but how she wished he could be more like their
father. Dad wasn't afraid to admit when he didn't know
something. In fact, he was always saying, "There's lots and
lots we can't explain. The world is full of mystery." Jenny
liked that. She liked living in a world full of mystery.

That night something else wonderful happened. After
the family had finished the turkey and dessert, they were
sitting around the table talking in the candlelight. Jenny's
tired eyes had begun to close, and as her lids started to touch,
everything glistened in the light of the candles. She gazed
through her lashes at her father and mother at opposite ends
of the table; Aunt Martha and Dennis and her cousin, Gerald, across from her; Uncle Ralph sitting next to her. Each
of the members of her family became blurry. But each was
glistening. It was as if rays of light were coming out from
them, rays that mixed together and connected. Her family looked, for a long moment, just like one huge, shining
snowflake!

22

chapter

✦ III ✦

It was the second Tuesday morning in January. Their father had left the day before to do consulting work in India. Jenny and Dennis were both getting dressed for school when their mother told them that there would be none. It had been canceled because a blizzard was supposed to hit before noon.

Jenny couldn't wait. "So there's going to be a lot of snow?" she asked her brother excitedly.

"A blizzard not only means a lot of snow," Dennis explained, "but also a lot of wind and cold way below freezing."

When Jenny went outside she found that hard to believe. Yes, it was cold but not *that* cold. Yes, there was a little wind coming from the east but not much. Yes, the sky was gray. But it was often gray during winter in New England. And there was not a single flake to be seen. Maybe it had been a mistake to cancel school.

Around ten o'clock, Jenny glanced out the window and saw that it had begun to snow. The flakes were small like Harry. But they weren't fluttering down as he had. They were coming in from the east, each one on a straight line as if it were in a hurry.

At first, there weren't all that many. Within fifteen minutes, however, there were lots of them. And Jenny noticed something strange. They were going sideways through the air. They didn't even seem to be landing on the ground. As she looked out the window, she watched them whip past the house from left to right. She was sorry they didn't want to stop, imagining they were just going to fly right by without ever coming to earth and leaving any snow to play in.

But she was mistaken. By eleven, the lawn was white, and she realized the fine flakes were moving so fast she simply couldn't see those that hit the ground. By noon, the snow was already an inch deep. "Hey, let's go sledding," she suggested to Dennis. He liked the idea enough to get up from the computer.

"Not until you have your lunch," said their mother, who had overheard them. "And then I want you to be dressed warmly; I want to know just where you are; and I don't want you to stay out long."

After lunch they took their saucer sleds and headed out to the path behind their house where it dipped down the hillside into the meadow. It was the best place nearby for sledding.

And what good sledding it was! The hard earth was now

covered with two inches of dry snow. Jenny and Dennis could slide fast all the way down the path twenty yards out into the meadow. But Jenny didn't enjoy herself for long. These snowflakes were not at all friendly like Harry. They stung her face like needles. And even though she could barely see them, they were so thick they made it hard for her to breathe. Now Jenny understood why her mother had wanted them to be so careful. "Let's go home," she said after a while. Dennis shrugged his shoulders. They had promised to be home at three o'clock, but they were back inside by two. Jenny spent the rest of the afternoon looking out the window. She couldn't make out any single flake, yet the house seemed to be surrounded by a fog. She couldn't even see the other side of the street. Minute by minute the snow on the lawn became deeper, as if it were somehow growing out of the ground. After dark, they watched pictures of the storm on television.

25

It was announced that the schools would be closed the next day, too. "The plows won't be able to get through until the afternoon," their mother explained. "Speaking of which, I'll need you both to help me shovel in the morning, so get a good night's rest."

Before she went to bed, Jenny turned on the light at the end of the driveway, watching a million sparkles a minute whipping past. While these blizzard flakes were not friendly like Harry, there was still something very beautiful about them. And their power. And the fact that the snow was over a foot deep around the lamp post. Just before she fell asleep, she lay in bed thinking there was also something beautiful about the crackling sound made by the tiny snow needles hitting the windowpane and the moan of the wind outside in the darkness.

The storm was over by the time Jenny awoke in the morning. The sky was still gray. The wind had died down, although there was still enough to lift swirls of snow on the lawn and in the street.

Right after breakfast, she and Dennis went outside with the two broad, flat shovels. The snow was much deeper in some places than in others. The plow had not come by yet, and in the street, the snow was about two feet. Across the lawn and the driveway, it was only one foot. But in the backyard, between the kitchen and the tool shed, it was *four* feet deep! It covered half the kitchen window and was as

26

deep as Jenny was tall. Dennis called it a snowdrift. The path they finally shoveled from the kitchen door to the tool shed was like a tunnel. It was exciting to have a tunnel in their own backyard!

Shoveling was also hard work. Even though the snow seemed light and fluffy, Jenny couldn't lift more than a foot of it at a time. Dennis couldn't do much better. If it took the two of them that much work to shovel just the driveway and one path, Jenny wondered, just think of how much energy it must have taken God to carry the whole storm!

When they were back inside, drinking hot cocoa with their mother at the kitchen table, Jenny raised the issue. "How much work do you think it took God to bring all the snow here?" she asked.

"God didn't bring the snow," Dennis proclaimed. "The storm did."

Jenny ignored him. "How much snow can a truck carry, Mom?" she asked.

"Well, let's see," their mother said, "it all depends on the size of the truck. A big dump truck is about ten feet wide and twenty feet long, and I guess it could hold snow about ten feet deep. So that would be ten times ten times twenty —around two thousand cubic feet."

"How much land does our house have?" Jenny asked.

"Two acres. Why?"

"How many dump trucks would it take to move two feet of snow from somewhere else to our house?"

"Good gracious, I don't know," their mother said.

At this Dennis came alive. "Wait a minute," he practically shouted. "I'll figure it out." He jumped up from the table and in a minute was back with a pad and pencil, his calculator, and the encyclopedia. "Let's see," he said. "First I have to convert acres to square feet. Here it is. There are forty-three thousand, five hundred sixty square feet in an acre. That means we own eighty-seven thousand square feet, rounding off. Multiply that times two to get cubic feet of snow, divide it by two thousand to get the number of trucks." He looked up with a big grin and announced, "It would take eighty-seven dump trucks!"

"Then how many dump trucks would it take to blanket all of New England with two feet of snow?" Jenny asked. *Blanket* was the word the television had used to describe what the storm had done.

Now her brother dove for the atlas to find the area of

the New England states. After a few moments of calculating, he looked up again at his mother and sister. "I had to round off some of the figures," he said proudly, "but it would take about one billion, seven hundred and fifty million trucks."

29

"Are there that many trucks in the world?" Jenny wondered.

Dennis thought for a moment. "Nope. Not nearly."

"So it would take more trucks than there are in the whole world just to bring this one storm to our little part of the country," Jenny mused. "God sure must be pretty powerful."

Dennis looked as if he'd been trapped. "I told you, God didn't bring the snow. It's all done by the atmosphere," he argued. "Then the rotation of the earth causes storms in the atmosphere to move. It just happens that way."

"It just happens," Jenny repeated. "I guess it's another of those accidents."

"Well, sort of," her brother said lamely.

"Well, is it sort of an accident that we just happen to live where the storms bring us snow and rain so that it's green all summer—and not in the desert?"

"Of course not, stupid," Dennis admitted. "But that doesn't mean there's a God to bring storms."

Jenny thought she saw a faint smile on their mother's face. She also thought it was time to drop the subject. She was glad her brother was so smart that he could give her the numbers she wanted. But that didn't mean he could understand the numbers any better than she. In fact, it was quite possible he didn't understand them *as well* as she could.

That night before she went to sleep, Jenny whispered, "Thank you, God, for bringing such a big storm. It was a lot of work. I love You."

Then she wondered. God was certainly good to them. But did God actually love *her?* He—or She—was important and powerful. How could God possibly care for just one person, particularly for a person as small and ordinary as herself? But then she remembered Harry. Harry had gone to the trouble to find her. *Maybe God was like that.* She didn't know how, but maybe. Maybe God could somehow be both in a giant storm and in a single little snowflake. "I love you, Harry," Jenny said as she was falling asleep. "And I love You too, God . . . I think."

30

chapter

♦ IV ♦

Their father came home in March. On the first
Saturday after his return, he told them all about
his trip to India and the two months he'd spent in its capital
city, New Delhi.

"Most of the people there are Hindus," he recounted.
"They believe in reincarnation."

"What's reincarnation?" Jenny asked.

"I know!" Dennis cried, jumping to explain. "It's a
belief that after a person dies his soul is reborn in another
body. The word comes from the Latin *carne,* which means
'flesh' or 'meat' or 'body.' That means I would be reborn
into another body after I die. Also, I would have been in
someone else's body before I was born. I would have had a
past life."

"Good explanation, Dennis," their father praised.
"How about you, Jenny? Do you know what a soul is?"

"Sure," she replied. "My soul is the part of me that's
most me. It's not my body. It's not something I can touch.
But it's terribly important. It's who I really am underneath."

"Another good explanation," their father beamed. "You guys are both pretty smart, aren't you?"

"Do you believe in reincarnation, Daddy?" Jenny asked.

Their father looked thoughtful. "I guess not," he said after a while. "I do believe each person has a soul, though. And I know that our souls live on after we die. But I don't know whether they live on in bodies. And I don't know whether they existed before we were conceived or born."

"How do you know that our souls live on after we die?" Jenny asked.

Now their father looked even more thoughtful. "That's a very big question," he finally replied. "In fact, it's so big I'm not going to answer it. You see, some questions are so big you shouldn't take anyone else's answer for them. It's better if you figure out your own. Often, I think that's why we're put here: to find some solutions for ourselves. I tell you what, though, I'd be delighted to listen to any answer *you* come up with."

At first her dad's answer was frustrating for Jenny. Then it was exciting to think she'd been put on earth to figure out big answers for herself. It was like being a detective.

Later, as her brother was sitting at the computer, she asked, "Do you believe in reincarnation, Dennis?"

"Nah. It can't be proved. I don't like to believe anything when there's no proof."

"Do you have a soul?" she asked him.

"Yeah, I think there's something more to me than just my body."

She thought so too. She also thought of teasing him by asking, "Can you prove it?" But that would only be teasing, and Jenny had something more important to learn from Dennis. "You know the pond down below the meadow? Some of the water goes up into the air, doesn't it? What do you call that?"

"Evaporation."

"Oh, yeah. Thanks. When the water evaporates from the pond and goes up into the sky, then what happens to it?"

This was the kind of question Dennis loved. "It's in droplets so small you can't see them. It's called vapor—you know, like steam. That's where the word *evaporate* comes from. Vapor is an invisible part of the air. When it rises and cools it condenses; that's what makes the clouds."

"Then what happens?" Jenny continued.

"It gets carried around and around the earth by the wind. Remember what I told you a couple of months ago about the atmosphere? When there's a storm in the atmosphere, some of it condenses even more than a cloud and falls to earth as rain. Or, if it's cold enough, snow."

"Does it fall back down into our pond?"

"No, silly. I told you it gets carried around. It may end up in somebody else's pond on the other side of the world. Like in India."

"It sounds a little like reincarnation to me," Jenny said.

Dennis looked at her crossly. "Don't be stupid. Rein-carnation—if there were such a thing—has to do with *souls*. Water molecules and raindrops don't have souls."

"Does *Bernie* have a soul?" Jenny shot back. Bernie was the family dog, of whom her brother was very fond.

Dennis was clearly uncomfortable. "Well, yes. Maybe. I don't know."

That was a first—for her brother to admit he didn't know something! "If the water fell into a pond in India," she went on, "wouldn't it evaporate from there, too? And then fall somewhere else? And after a while, wouldn't it evaporate again and maybe fall right back into our pond?"

"It's possible," Dennis said. He sounded dubious. "But we're not talking about the same raindrop, you know. We're talking about the tiniest part of a raindrop—or snowflake—a molecule." Dennis nodded his head. "Yeah, if we're talk-ing about a single molecule of water—yeah, it's possible

34

that water molecule could end up right back in our pond."

Now Dennis could hardly stop talking. He was no longer doubtful. "In fact," he continued, "molecules are so small—there's a zillions times zillions of them—it's said that if you take a bucket of water out of the ocean, it would contain at least one molecule that was once in the body of every person who ever lived. Yeah, as long as you're talking about molecules, I guess some of them will come back here."

Jenny had everything she needed to know for the moment. "Thanks, Dennis," she said. "I'm going for a walk. Is it okay if I take Bernie?"

"Sure," her brother replied, turning back to the computer.

She was going for a long walk—down to the pond on the other side of the meadow. It was surprising how warm it was when she stepped outside. She didn't need her parka, only her sweater and boots. She knew that it wouldn't be the first day of spring until next week, but today it seemed that spring had already started. There was still about an inch of snow on the ground, but it looked old, with some higher ridges alongside the road that were almost black with dirt. Running down each side of the road, there was a tiny rivulet of melting snow. The sky was soft blue, and she could hear the sounds of birds.

"I think you've got a soul," Jenny said to Bernie as they started down the street. "So I don't see why a raindrop shouldn't have a soul." She went on thinking, "I'm not sure about reincarnation, but maybe everything has a soul.

36

Anyway, I *know*
that Harry has a soul."
Soon Jenny was at the bottom
of the hill by the little stream that
ran through a wide drainpipe underneath
the road. Often, it was dry. Today it was
full. The rivulets of melting snow on the sides of
the road were trickling into it. No wonder the stream looked
even more full where it came out of the culvert than where
it went in. The land was flowing with water today.

Jenny turned off the road and trudged through the wet
snow following the stream into the pine trees. There, a
smaller stream coming in from the meadow joined it. She
followed the now larger stream, thinking of a picture in Dennis's encyclopedia. It was a diagram of the veins going to the
heart. It showed how the little veins joined together to form
bigger veins and the bigger veins joined to form even bigger
veins. Maybe the streams were like veins, and the earth was
like a body. Maybe the whole earth was alive.

Twenty yards farther, the stream gushed into Babcock

Pond. Sometimes Jenny thought it ought to be called Babcock Lake. It was at least three times the size of their own property. That meant it was more than six acres.

All winter the pond had been covered with ice and snow. Jenny had walked across it a week after the blizzard. She wouldn't do that today, though. She knew the ice was no longer thick enough to hold her.

So she walked around the pond to the dam at the other end. Sometimes there was no water flowing over it. Now, just as she suspected, water was pouring through the four-foot-wide cut in the dam, forming a waterfall that plummeted into Babcock Brook.

38

Jenny sat down on the side of the dam. It was in the sun. She enjoyed feeling the warmth seeping through her sweater. She gazed on where the brook rushed out of sight through the woods fifty yards downstream. She knew that Babcock Brook ran into Morse's River just outside the village two miles away. And she knew that Morse's River flowed into the Connecticut River. And that the Connecticut River fed into the Atlantic Ocean. All streams flowed into brooks, and all brooks into rivers, and all rivers into the ocean. She thought again of the picture of the veins leading to the heart. Maybe the ocean was like the heart of the earth.

She looked back at the water pouring over the dam and thought about Harry. Harry had evaporated off the tip of her nose and gone back into the sky. Then he would have fallen someplace else, like the ocean. And someplace else. But maybe after four months of traveling all around the world he had fallen right back into Babcock Pond. In fact, he might be part of the melting ice and snow right here. He could be flowing over the dam this very minute!

Jenny followed the ripples of the brook beneath her until they vanished between the trees. "Good-bye, Harry!" she shouted and waved her hand. "I'll see you again next year!"